The story of Noah and the Ark

Retold by ROBERT MATHIAS

Illustrated by MAGGIE DOWNER

Derrydale Books

NEW YORK

A TEMPLAR BOOK

This 1992 edition published by Derrydale Books,
distributed by Outlet Book Company, Inc., a Random House Company,
225 Park Avenue South, New York, New York 10003.

Devised and produced by The Templar Company plc,
Pippbrook Mill, London Road, Dorking, Surrey RH4 1JE, Great Britain.

Edited by Wendy Madgwick
Designed by Janie Louise Hunt
Printed and bound in Malaysia

ISBN 0-517-06729-3
87654321

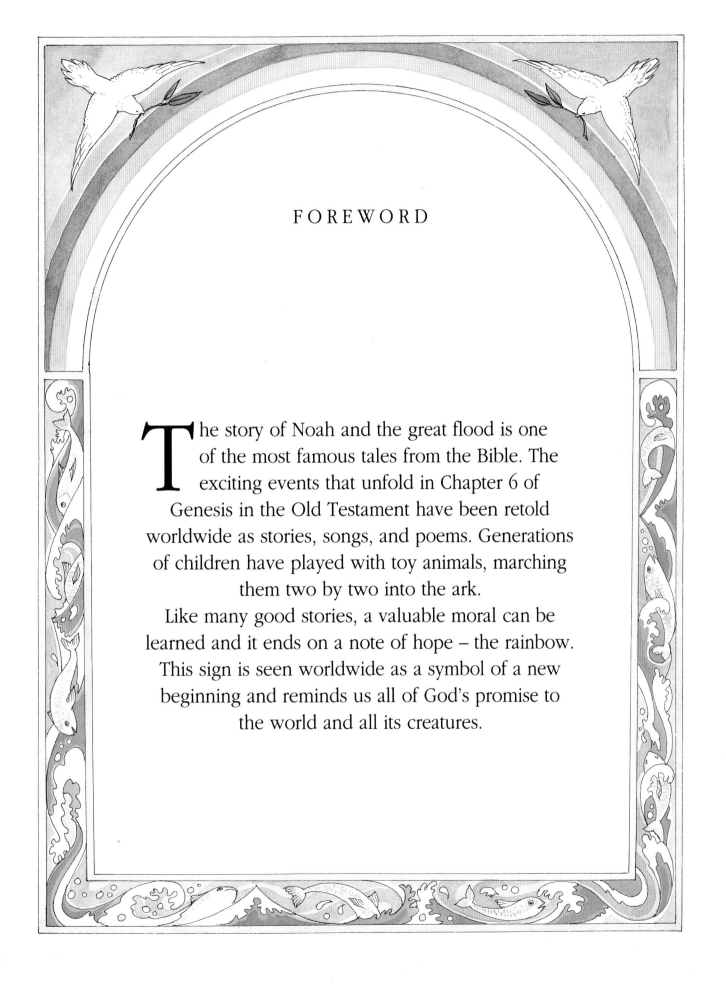

FOREWORD

The story of Noah and the great flood is one of the most famous tales from the Bible. The exciting events that unfold in Chapter 6 of Genesis in the Old Testament have been retold worldwide as stories, songs, and poems. Generations of children have played with toy animals, marching them two by two into the ark.

Like many good stories, a valuable moral can be learned and it ends on a note of hope – the rainbow. This sign is seen worldwide as a symbol of a new beginning and reminds us all of God's promise to the world and all its creatures.

Long ago when the world was young the Lord God looked upon it and sadly shook his head. Across the land he could see only evil and wickedness. Wherever he looked he saw men cheating, stealing, and lying to each other. They were greedy for wealth and power and paid no heed to His teachings.

"I will end this evil," He thought. "I will send rain to flood the earth and cleanse it of all that is evil and wicked."

But God noticed one man who stood alone among the crowds and who followed the path of goodness. He was an honest and truthful man who respected all around him. His name was Noah. Noah prayed every day and tried to lead a good life and follow God's teaching. God looked on Noah with favor.

One day, Noah slowly made his way along the crowded street. He was sadder than he had ever been

before, for thieves had set on him and taken all his hard-earned goods. At last he reached his home and opened the door.

"Dear wife," he sighed. "I fear we have no reward for our labors. I have been robbed and all our our work has been in vain."

Noah's wife came swiftly to his side and took his hand in hers. She led him to the table where his three sons, Shem, Ham, and Japheth, were sitting with their three good wives.

"Come, my dear, eat with us. We can labor again tomorrow. It is God's will that this has happened – perhaps those thieves had greater need than us." Hearing her wise words, Noah smiled again and sat to eat his meal.

The next day, the soft morning sunshine filled Noah's tiny garden. He knelt beneath a shady tree, his lean, brown hands folded in prayer. Seeing him there, God spoke to him.

"Noah, I am going to send a great flood to rid the earth of evil. No man who follows the path of sin shall live. But you and your family are good people, Noah. I have seen this and for this reason I have chosen you to carry out a great and important task."

Noah remained silent as the Lord continued.

"You must build an ark, a great vessel made of gopher wood. It must be 300 cubits long, 50 cubits wide, and 30 cubits high. Furnish it with decks and

many chambers and make a window and a doorway in its side. When it is complete, take your wife and sons and their wives into it." God paused for a second and then continued.

"With you, you must take two animals, a male and a female, of every creature that lives upon the earth. Big and small, fierce and gentle, beautiful and ugly – you must ensure they all are there. And you will need food and water too, enough for all on board. Then, when the rains come, you will be saved from destruction."

Noah gasped at the thought of such a task, but he nodded. He would do as God had commanded.

Later, Noah told his family what the Lord had said to him.

"Dear husband," said his wife, "we must start work at once."

Shem and Ham were silent, their faces anxious. But Japheth, his brow knitted in thought, asked:

"Gopher wood, father? What kind of wood is that?" Noah smiled at his innocent question and pointed through the open window.

"There, on the hillside, those tall cypress trees that stand strong against the blast of the winds and the heat of the sun – that is gopher wood."

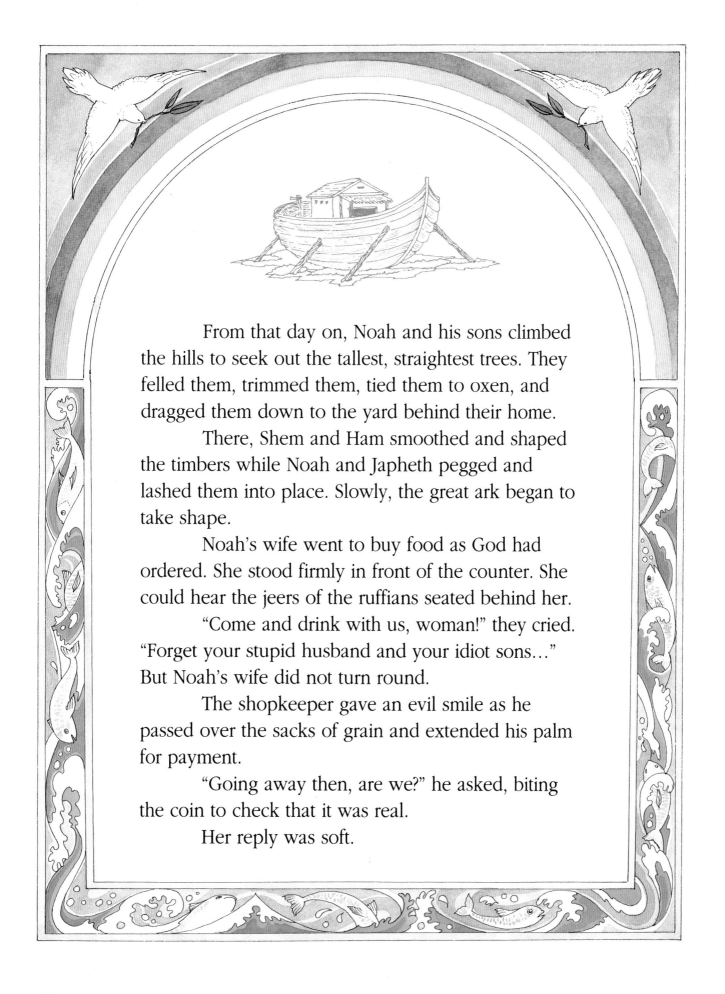

From that day on, Noah and his sons climbed the hills to seek out the tallest, straightest trees. They felled them, trimmed them, tied them to oxen, and dragged them down to the yard behind their home.

There, Shem and Ham smoothed and shaped the timbers while Noah and Japheth pegged and lashed them into place. Slowly, the great ark began to take shape.

Noah's wife went to buy food as God had ordered. She stood firmly in front of the counter. She could hear the jeers of the ruffians seated behind her.

"Come and drink with us, woman!" they cried. "Forget your stupid husband and your idiot sons…" But Noah's wife did not turn round.

The shopkeeper gave an evil smile as he passed over the sacks of grain and extended his palm for payment.

"Going away then, are we?" he asked, biting the coin to check that it was real.

Her reply was soft.

"Bless you and thank you," she said, and turned to walk between the sneering men. Soon she was leading her donkey away from the store, climbing the stony path towards her home.

"Only a few more sacks of grain and we shall have enough food to see us through," she murmured.

The framework of the ark rose higher and higher and soon it towered over the roof of Noah's house. The time had come for his sons to travel far

and wide, seeking out every living creature throughout the lands of the earth.

"And remember," said Noah, wagging his finger at them as they left. "Let not a single creature be forgotten, no matter how small or how large. Bring two of each, a male and a female to go with us into the ark."

So, armed with ropes, nets, snares, boxes, jars, and cages, the three brothers set out on their quest.

While they were away Noah and the four wives worked from dawn to dusk. They built pens and stalls to house the animals. They baked and bottled all kinds of different foods. They packed dates and figs and put peppers to dry in the sun. They filled stone jars with spring water and corked and waxed them to seal them tight. Hay was stacked in great bundles and birdseed shaken down in canvas bags. Soon, all the provisions for their needs were gathered.

The first son to return was Ham. Behind him,
as he rode up to the house, stretched a caravan of a
thousand camels, each one laden with a hundred
cages. In each cage perched birds of every size, shape,
and color.

In twos they hopped and fluttered. Huge
yellow-billed toucans shifted and swayed; jeweled
humming-birds whirred in a flurry of feathers; jet-eyed
ravens stared and strutted; parrots preened; geese
gabbled; and starlings swaggered. Only the wise old
owls sat still and silent in their cage, watching all that
happened with a knowing air.

It seemed that every bird that ever flew in the air or strutted on the ground was held in the cages strung from the camels' backs. The unloading began, but it was long into the night before the camel drivers took their leave.

To the taunting town's folk, the great ark was just a joke.

"Only a fool mistakes the desert for a beach!" said one.

"Are you going to sail the sands, then, Noah?" shouted another.

Noah ignored their ridicule and worked even harder. The decks of the ark were sealed and the chambers for the animals were ready. The windows were cut and a doorway yawned in the vessel's side. Each was fitted with a strong shutter to keep out the waters of the flood. Only one task remained – to paint the hull with pitch.

Noah lit a fire beneath a huge cauldron and threw in the toffee-black pitch. It bubbled and popped as he stirred it with a long pole, and smoke billowed from the thick, molten liquid. Noah looked up, puzzled – it seemed to him that the smoke was darkening the sky. But he was wrong! The sky itself was dark with rain for as far as he could see. Despite the heat of the fire, Noah shivered as he thought of what was to come.

Japeth was next to return and Shem followed
four days later. Between them they had gathered all
the animals of the world, just one pair of each, a male
and a female.

Around the ark the pens and stalls, cages and
baskets were full. And as Noah watched them he saw
that a strange thing had happened. Fierce lions and
tigers rested next to antelopes and deer, closing their
golden eyes as Shem patted their muzzles. The hyena
slept quietly by the side of the zebra and a crocodile
dozed next to a tiny lamb. The coiled cobra kept its
venom from the chattering monkeys.

The checkered giraffe, the mighty ape, the
timid mouse, the bouncy kangaroo, the horned
rhinoceros, the leopard and the lemur, the lemming
and the snow bear – all were at peace with one another.

The skies grew darker still and it was time for
the animals to enter the ark. Aided by his three sons,
Noah dragged a huge ramp up to the ark and placed it
close to the great doorway.

For days and nights the creatures stepped up
two by two. The lumbering elephants, trunks swinging,
bent the mighty ramp with their great weight. The
bison and the wildebeest snorted and their hooves

clattered on the gopher wood, while the camels trod
with a measured pace up the great ramp of the ark.

Small creatures like mice and moles, butterflies
and bees, worms and weevils, scorpions and spiders,
snails and slugs, turtles and toads, and all the banded
writhing snakes – all of these, and a thousand others,
were lifted into the ark by Noah and his wife, his
three sons, and their good wives.

"There are no more," sighed Noah at last,
wiping his brow. But a movement stirred his cloak
and, at his feet, a cat and his mate purred silently by.

Now God came and spoke to Noah again.

"Noah, from this day on it will rain for forty days and forty nights. Take your family into the ark with all the creatures of the earth that you have gathered. There, you will be safe from the flood."

Noah closed the door of the ark as, outside, the leaden sky grew darker. Daggers of lightning flashed against the billowing clouds as slowly, slowly it began to rain.

Two men arguing in the road below cursed as the first raindrops spattered their faces. More drops fell, each puffing dust as it struck the parched earth, then seeping and spreading like a darkened flower-head to join its neighbor. Soon, the road was awash with rivulets of gurgling water.

People covered their heads as they splashed through the downpour, stumbling to reach their homes. Once there, they watched in horror as the rain pounded through their flimsy roofs and washed down the walls. They climbed up to their sleeping chambers as the waters gushed around their feet and turned the floors to mud.

And less than an hour had passed since the rains began.

"Quick, let us find that fool Noah, and steal his boat!" said one man.

"We'll hurl him into the mud!" added another.

Soon a procession of men and women, clutching at each other, were scrambling along the road to Noah's house, but before long there was no longer a road, just a raging torrent of tumbling yellow water. All around, the mud-brick houses were crumbling, their sodden walls melting into the ever-rising waters. They called to Noah but all he could hear was the constant beat of the rain.

Noah listened to the roar of the waters and prayed beneath the pounding of the raindrops. Through his window he watched the rain slicing down like the blades of a million swords. Black thunder

clouds hurled themselves angrily across the sky and the wind screeched above him. The rushing waters lashing the mighty ark sounded like a thousand waterfalls.

Suddenly, the ark lurched. Noah heard the logs beneath it grind and splinter as the huge three-storied ark floated free. Spinning and rolling, it was carried away on the raging torrent.

Noah watched from his window for many days. First the ark rose above the treetops. Then the hills and finally the mountaintops slipped below the waves and vanished from sight.

Now the whole earth was covered by water. Just as God had said, the rains thundered down for forty days and forty nights. The ark was tossed by huge waves and tilted by screaming gales that made the gopher timbers creak and groan, but all within the ark was calm.

Then, one night, Noah woke with a start. What sound had woken him? He listened… then he realized – it was quiet! The rain had stopped and the ark was floating on still waters. He listened again, thinking he must be dreaming, but the only sound was the soft lapping of the water playing around the hull.

Noah could no longer sleep and sat close to the window to wait for the dawn. When it came, Noah smiled. It did not rise as usual with angry clouds, black and swollen, pressing down on the waters. It lifted softly, the darkness fading to pale pinks and jades, like an azure veil.

"Thank you, God," cried Noah, and he watched as the tip of the sun rose above the watery horizon.

Thereafter each dawn was more beautiful than the last. The sun gained strength and warmed the hearts of all on board. Noah opened the window and the soft morning breeze wafted through the ark.

The great vessel drifted peacefully along as the sparkling waters covering the earth slowly receded. After many days the ark glided to a stop. It came to rest with a gentle bump against the top of a mountain called Ararat.

Immediately, Noah let a raven fly free from the window. All day he waited, searching the skies for the bird, but it did not return. On the following day he released a dove, and again he waited and watched.

Eventually he saw it flapping feebly back, exhausted. It had found no land on which to rest. Noah took it tenderly back inside the ark and placed it with its mate.

Seven more days went by before he took the second dove and set it free again. Again he waited and that evening, to his joy, the bird returned. In its beak it carried the leaves from an olive tree.

From this sign Noah knew that the waters covering the earth were falling. Soon, he and his family would be able to leave the ark.

A warm wind, sent by God, sprang up to dry the land and drive the waters back to the oceans. Trees began to appear above the waves. As the days passed and the land dried, wild plants emerged and flowered in the warm sunshine.

At last God spoke again to Noah:

"It is time for you to leave the ark," He said. "Take with you your wife and your sons, and the wives of your sons. Take also every beast and bird

and reptile and all the other creatures that are within
the ark. Go on to the earth and set them free. Let them
spread across the land to breed and multiply and fill
the earth with life."

So Noah and his wife and his three sons,
Shem, Ham, and Japheth, and their good wives left the
ark and returned to the land. All the creatures they
had taken with them were released to roam far and
wide, in freedom as they pleased.

Above the ark the sparkling sky was full of birds, calling, wheeling and darting, diving and swooping, as they scattered across the many lands of the earth.

Beneath the ark the mice made a nest and the scorpion scuttled beneath a rock to shelter from the sun. The crab stepped sideways to the safety of the sea and the lizard, cool and yawning, basked on the sand.

On the plains, the bison stamped and butted, while the leopards searched for a shady place in which to lie. In the forests monkeys chattered once again and bears blinked in the warm sunshine.

Several months passed and the flood dried up. Every day Noah and his family went to the altar they had built to God on the mountainside and gave thanks for their safety and good fortune.

Noah and his wife were content. They looked out across to the nearby hillside where stood their tiny house. They waved at the small figures of Shem and his wife tending their flock of goats in the valley below. They looked down across the fields and waved

again at Ham who was helping his wife plant a garden close to their home. Lastly they looked to see their third son and smiled when they saw him. Japheth

danced and played on his flute to the delight of his wife and their children, who chuckled and clenched their fists to their lips.

Noah smiled. He rested his arm across the shoulders of his dear wife and drew her closer to him.

Away to the west the pale curve of a rainbow rose from the earth, tinting an arc across the sky, and Noah remembered God's words to him after the flood.

"Noah, I will make an agreement with you and with your children, and your children's children. Never again shall there be a flood to destroy the earth. And the sign of this is a rainbow. Whenever rain and sun appear in the sky, a rainbow will occur in the cloud to remind everyone of my promise."

At this thought, Noah bowed his head in prayer.

"Thank you, God," he murmured.